# What Do I Really Want To Achieve?

# How to Use These Cards

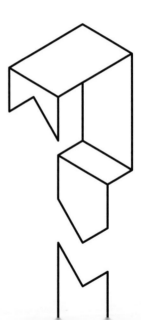

This box contains 160 cards that represent possible goals and priorities.

There are 140 goals and priorities arranged into 10 categories, corresponding to the areas of life we all need to focus on in order to find fulfilment: BODY, FAMILY, FRIENDSHIP/SOCIABILITY, LEISURE, LOVE, MEANING, MONEY, MOOD, SELF and WORK.

We've also included 20 blank cards, so you can write down any goals or priorities that aren't included in this set.

In this booklet, you'll find six exercises for using the cards. Don't feel obliged to use any of them: you might just want to arrange the cards yourself according to whatever order comes to mind. However, we have designed the exercises to give you a means of selecting and organising your goals, helping you determine which are the most important, urgent, realistic or meaningful, so that you can establish a plan for achieving or prioritising those you choose.

Once chosen, the cards can be used however you see fit. You might find it useful to keep them close at hand, perhaps tucked into a purse or wallet, pinned to a noticeboard, or photographed on your phone, as a reminder of where you are truly headed.

# Pyramid of
# Psychological Needs

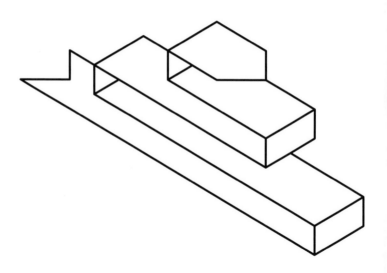

This exercise is based on Maslow's pyramid of needs, as designed by the psychologist Abraham Maslow. He attempted to create a unified theory of human motivation by categorising the different kinds of needs we all share, and demonstrating the order in which they must be met.

At the bottom, he placed our more basic needs: our *physiological* needs (like food, water, warmth and rest); and our *safety* needs (like security and physical safety). Understandably, it's these that must be met first, since they are crucial for survival.

The upper part he reserved for our psychological needs: our need for *love and belonging*; our desire for *esteem*; and finally, our yearning for *self-actualisation*.

Since most of us are already meeting our basic needs, almost all of our goals and priorities represent our efforts to meet these three psychological needs; satisfying them means the difference between merely surviving and living. Maslow's pyramid is no dry psychological tool: it represents a roadmap for fulfilment.

Arrange your cards into a three-tiered pyramid that represents your psychological needs.

1. Along the bottom row, choose three or four cards from the LOVE, FAMILY or FRIENDSHIP/SOCIABILITY categories that fulfil your need for *love and belonging* – those that relate to your intimate relationships, whether with friends, family, colleagues or romantic partners.

2. In the middle row, choose two to three cards from the WORK, MONEY, MOOD or BODY categories that fulfil your need for *esteem* – those that relate to your need to gain prestige and feel a sense of accomplishment with your efforts.

3. In the top row, choose one or two cards from the SELF, LEISURE and MEANING categories that support your need for *self-actualisation* – those that relate to your need to achieve your full potential and fulfil your life's purpose.

| Becoming more emotionally mature | Finding my life's purpose |

SELF-ACTUALISATION

| Earning more money | Lose weight | Finding calm |

ESTEEM

| Spending more time with the children | Reconnecting with old friends | Settling down | Having deeper, more meaningful conversations |

LOVE AND BELONGING

# Priority Planner

Our goals and priorities are not uniform: they require differing amounts of effort, and different timeframes in which they can be achieved. Some are short term: with a little judicious effort, they may be accomplished in the space of a week or so. Others can only be achieved over a much longer period: a matter not of weeks, but months, or years – perhaps even a lifetime. Yet this is usually a sign of their true importance. Ultimately, our longer-term goals are those which will bring us the greatest degree of fulfilment. In the future, when we look back on our lives, it is these we will feel the most pride and satisfaction in having worked towards and achieved.

Once you've selected a number of goals and priorities you wish to work towards, arrange them according to the time you expect it will take you to achieve them. Sort those you feel can be accomplished...

1. This week
2. This month
3. This year
4. Within five years
5. Over a lifetime

Use this planner as a guide as to how to tackle your goals and priorities, and a reminder of the time it will take to achieve your most treasured ambitions.

| THIS WEEK | THIS MONTH | THIS YEAR | NEXT FIVE YEARS | OVER A LIFETIME |
|---|---|---|---|---|
| More exercise | Reading more | Finding a partner | Paying off the mortgage | Finding my life's purpose |
| Less drinking | More parties | Opening up to my friends | Marriage | Starting a family |

# Tournament of Priorities

Though almost all of us can identify areas of our lives we would like to improve, it is often hard to decide where we should place our focus. Ideally, we would achieve perfection across the board, but since our time is short, we need to identify where it will be best spent. This is an exercise to help you decide which of your goals is the most important to you.

Stage a tournament of priorities. First, choose 8–10 possible goals and priorities from a particular category you feel you would like to work towards. Then sort them into pairs and pit them against each other, eliminating whichever one you feel you could live without achieving. Advance from the quarter-finals to the semi-finals and then on to the final itself.

Ultimately, you should arrive at a single champion goal: the one you are most invested in meeting. At the same time, you'll be left with a number of close runners-up to tackle once your champion has been achieved.

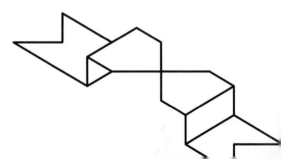

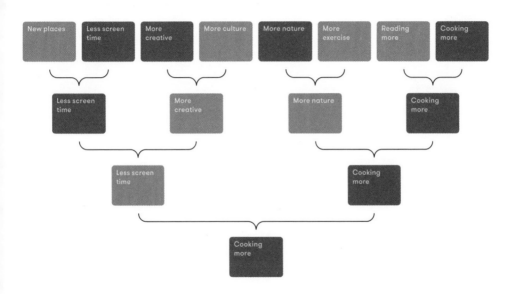

# Steps to Fulfilment

A common pitfall when setting goals for ourselves is over-ambition. We set our sights on a lofty target and fall into despair when it appears beyond our capabilities. The solution is not to give up, but to refocus. Keeping our ultimate goal in mind, we should train our sights on smaller, more achievable goals that will help us take steps towards attaining it.

First, select an ultimate goal from a particular category: an ambitious target you would like to reach but are currently some way off from achieving. Next, search through the deck and select any other goal or priority that will help you move towards this ultimate goal – ones that will give you the necessary skills, means, opportunities and experiences to progress.

Arrange your chosen cards into a set of discrete, sequential steps. This will provide you with a defined and achievable programme with which to begin advancing towards your ultimate ambition, wherein you can feel pride and progress with every step you take.

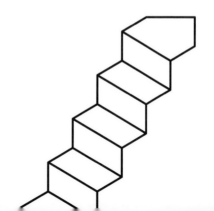

Earning money from my passion

Finding a partner

Working out real interests

Having deeper, more meaningful conversations

More creative

Talking to more strangers

Wasting less money

More parties

Less screen time

Understanding myself better

# The Feasibility-Fulfilment Matrix

Our goals and priorities can be measured on different axes. One might be *feasibility*. A goal of procrastinating less will be easier to achieve than that of starting our own business, for example. Another is *fulfilment*. Ultimately, we will gain greater total satisfaction from reading a novel than we will from watching television, say. This is an exercise to help you plot your goals on both these axes as a way of deciding which to prioritise.

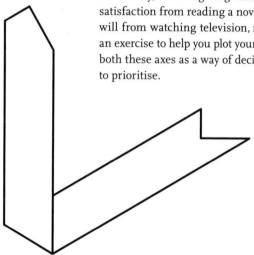

Make a selection of 10 or so cards, either from a single category or a sample from different categories you wish to focus on.

1. Those that are not very feasible and only somewhat fulfilling are *inessential*, and probably not worth your time and effort.

2. Those that are highly feasible but only somewhat fulfilling are *nice to have*. They shouldn't demand your full focus, but may still be worth attempting.

3. Those that are not very feasible but highly fulfilling are *distant dreams*. These will likely require a lot of time, effort (and luck) to achieve. They are worth aiming for, but the scale of the challenge should be kept in mind: you shouldn't be too hard on yourself if you fail to achieve them.

4. Those that are very feasible and highly fulfilling are *achievable ambitions*. These should be your highest priority: they offer the most guaranteed route to fulfilment.

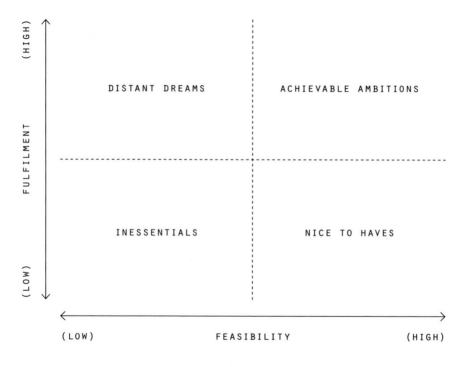

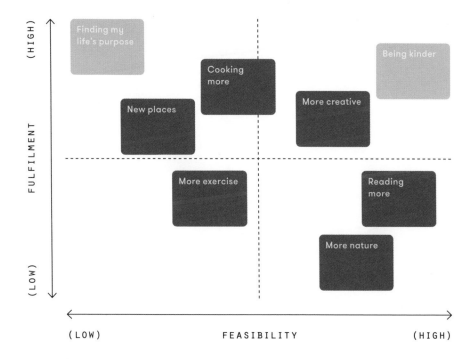

# Wallet, Nightstand and Phone

Given how hectic and distracting our days can be, it's useful to remind ourselves of our higher goals and priorities by displaying them where you will notice them. There are many possibilities for placing a helpful reminder in your eyeline – a particular BODY card might be worth displaying on the fridge, for example. But here's one suggestion we think is useful: the Wallet, Nightstand and Phone display.

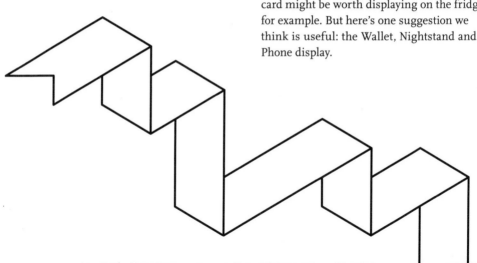

Pick three cards from any category.

1. Keep one card in your wallet or purse. This should be one you need to constantly remember; a goal or priority you wish to always keep to the forefront of your mind (perhaps in the SELF, LOVE, FAMILY or MEANING categories). By carrying it about with you everywhere you go (like a photo of a child or a loved one), it becomes a physical reminder of what truly matters.

2. Leave one card on your nightstand or bedside table. This should be a goal or priority you wish to be reminded of, at either the beginning or the end of each day, that can be worked on first thing in the morning or just before you go to sleep (perhaps related to the MIND, BODY or MOOD category).

3. Take a photo of one priority and have it as the backdrop on your phone (or somewhere prominent in it). You'll be regularly nudged towards your true aspiration.

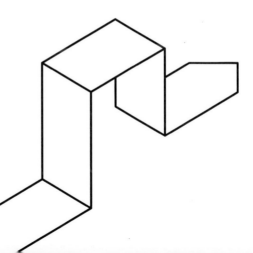

Scan to join our community:

THE SCHOOL OF LIFE is a global organisation helping people lead more fulfilled lives. It is a resource for helping us understand ourselves, for improving our relationships, our careers and our social lives – as well as for helping us find calm and get more out of our leisure hours. We offer a range of books, gifts and stationery which is available worldwide.

THESCHOOLOFLIFE.COM